NATIVE AMERICAN AFFILIATE PROGRAMS

Compiled by GWFT

DISCLAIMER

The material and information contained in this booklet is for general information purposes only. You should not rely upon the material or information as a basis for making business, legal or other decisions.

"Disclosure: We are affiliates of Bookshop.org and will earn a commission if you click through and make a purchase."

We are also affiliates of selected other programs and receive a commission when you click through the links.

Affiliate marketing enables members to earn revenue on sales made to customers who click on referral links.

For further information on Affiliate marketing and its history go to:

https://en.wikipedia.org/wiki/Affiliate_marketing

And this free publication:

The Ultimate Affiliate Marketing Guide: A Free Step-by-Step for Beginners

https://www.affiliateprograms.com/affiliate-marketing

And

https://www.affiliateprograms/how-affiliate-marketing-works

Set up your own free Native American Bookshop. Promote your favorite books and authors. Advertise your own books free.

https://bookshop.org/shop/mybookstore

https://bookshop.org/lists/native-american-books-and-authors

CHILDREN OF NATIVE AMERICA TODAY

https://bookshop.org/a/19693/9781570919657

Share your favorite books through Bookshop's free affiliate program

Curate your own list of Native American books and authors. Promote your own writings.

Custom design your own products and gifts here. Set up your own free store:

ZAZZLE

https://www.zazzle.com/s/native+american?rf=2388822630 69250577

"Shop & create on Zazzle."

What is Affiliate marketing?

Affiliate programs offer affiliates a way to earn money online to profit from their websites and blogs. Some affiliate programs do not require a website, and there are many providers of free business and personal websites.

Affiliate programs are free to join. You should never pay a fee to join an affiliate program. Many of our listed affiliate programs are easy for beginners. There are both individual affiliate programs and affiliate networks where you can find mahny affiliate opportunities in many niche areas. Some allow you to set up your own storefronts.

Check out these websites for affiliate programs of specific interest to Native Americans and to affiliate with Native American companies and Naive American made products:

NATIVE AMERICAN WHOLESALE

https://www.nativeamericanwholesale.com/index.php?route=affiliate/login

NATIVE AMERICAN PASSIONS

https://natiaveamericanpassions.com/deinfo/Affiliate-Programs.html

NATIVE AMERICAN TEA

https://www.nativeamericantea.com/join-=our-aqfffiliate-program

INDIGENOUS DESIGNS

https://indigenous.com/pages/affiliate

OTHER NATIVE AMERICAN WEBSITES OF INTEREST:

NATIVE REMEDIES

https://www.nativeremedies.com/native-remedies-affiliate-signup.html

NATIVE MEDIA NETWORK

https://www.nativemedianetwork.com

NATIVE AMERICAN BUSINESS DIRECTORY

https://nativebusinessdirectory.com

"#1 source for finding American Indian owned & Native American owned businesses"

CHANGING HANDS

https://www.changinghands.com/page/native-american-indigenous-ownvoices-books

MY POWWOW STORE

https://www.mypowwowstore.com

POWWOWS.COM

https://www.powwows.com

FIRST NATIONS PRODUCTS AT AMAZON

https://amzn.to/2OC6EiN

https://amzn.to/3qtwJy7

https://amzn.to/38lwnmQ

https://amzn.to/3bpVHtF

INDIAN STORE

https://indianstore.org

INDIANS.ORG

https://indians.org/articles/native-american-products.html

Wide assortment of clothing, jewelry, musical instruments, artifacts, etc.

THE GOOD TRADE

https://www.thegoodtrade.com/features/native-owned-brands-to-support

LIVING DRUMS

https://www.livingdrums.com

MADE IN NEW MEXICO

https://madeinnewmexzico.com/products/native-american

UNDER ONE NATION

https://underonenationtribetradingpost.net

ETSY MARKET

https://www.etsy.com/market/native_american_made

NAIVE AMERICAN TODAY

https://nativeamericantoday.com/gifts-novelties

NATIVE AMERICAN WORLD

https://nativeamericanworld.net

INDIAN GIFTS

https://www.indiangifts.com

For more native owned and native made products, put in search engine:

SHOP NATIVE

SHOP NATIVE AMERICAN MADE PRODUCTS

NATIVE AMERICAN PRODUCTS AND GIFTS

WHERE AND HOW TO ADVERTISE YOUR AFFILIATE PROGRAMS AND AFFILIATE LINKS

Free Promotions Page

http://trafficg.com/my-promotions.php?member=gwft

Oboads

https://www.oboads.com

ENTIREWEB.COM

https://www.entireweb.com/free_submission/?a=fnbpublica

FREE UNLIMITED ROTATOR

http://freerotator.com/ro/?r=3&u=GWFT

Browse this rotator for links to more Native American products and affiliate programs. Sign up for your own free unlimited rotator.

If you do not have a website or blog, free websites or blog, free websites or blogs can be obtained here:

WEBSTARTS

https://www.Webstarts.com/?aff=GWFT

WEBS.COM

https://www.webs.com

ALL4WEBS

https://www.All4Webs.com/fnbpublica/home/hlm

WIX

https://www/wix/ecommerce/website

WEEBLY

https://www.weebly.com

TOP 5 WEBSITE BUILDERS

https://www/top5-websitebuilders.com/make_website

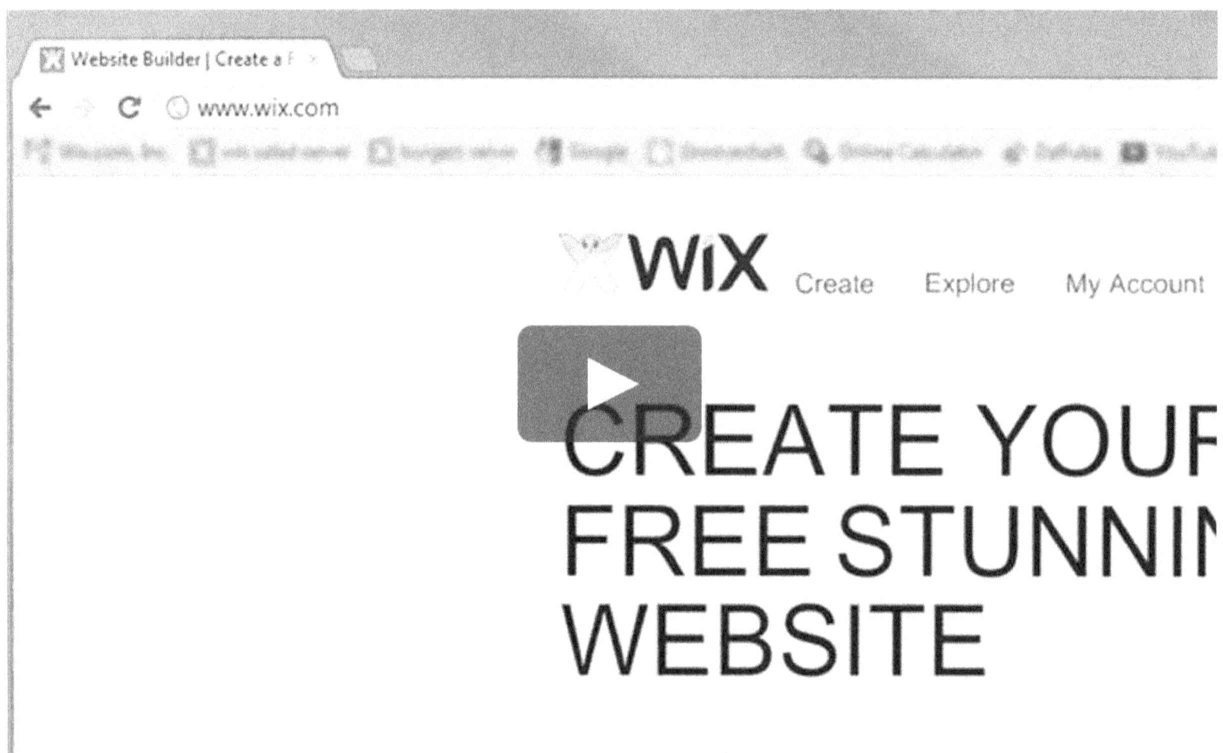

CLICKBANK AFFILIATE PROGRAM

Sell digital products

http://fnbpublica.reseller.hop.clickbank.net

CJ.com

Established affiliate marketing network

https://www.cj.com

https://cj.com/what-is-affiliate-marketing

LINKCONNECTOR

"Join the linkconnector network. Got traffic? Get paid. Earn money from your website traffic!"

https://www.linkconnector.com/ta.php?lc=004268000078001435

ECOMMERCE AFFILIATE NETWORK

More than 1800 affiliate programs across 21 product categories--Free to join with generous commissions paid; browse their most popular affiliate programs; feature your own affiliate program

https://e-commerceaffiliates.com

SHAREASALE

https://www.shareasale.com

OTHER WEBSITES OF INTEREST

https://www.allproducts.web

HOW TO PROMOTE AFFILIATE LINKS WEBSITES

https://convertkit.com/how-to-promote-affiliate-links

https://marketartfully.com/how-to-do-affiliate-marketing-for-free-without-paying-for-ads

https://www.bigcreative.com/blog/affiliate-income-tips

https://www.marketingdigibook.com/blog/affiliate-marketing-tips

FOR FURTHER AFFILIATE MARKETING TIPS

PUT IN SEARCH ENGINE

How to Promote Affiliate Links

Where to Promote Affiliate Links

How to Build a Successful Affiliate Marketing Site

Free Advertising

Sign up for an Amazon Affiliate Program to sell Native American products on Amazon

https://affiliate-program.amazon.com

PUBLISH YOUR AFFILIATE BOOKS AND EBOOKS FREE

https://kdp.amazon.com

https://kdp.amazon.com/en_US/l/print-on-demand

https://www.thebookpatch.com

https://www.lulu.com

https://www.bookrix.com

https://www.blurb.com/self-publishing

https://selfpublish.sweek.com

https://press/barnesandnoble.com

FREE BOOK COVER TEMPLATES

AFFILIATE MARKETING BOOKS

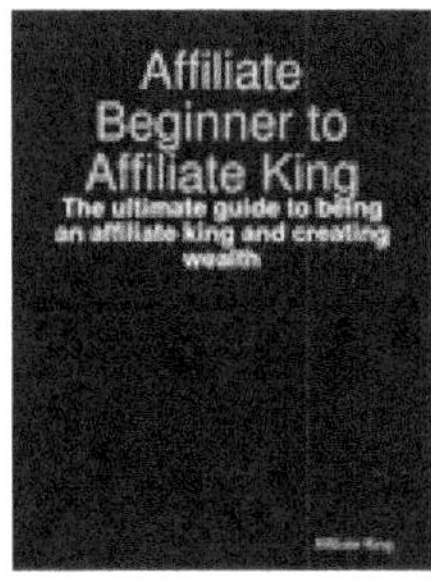

For additional affiliate marketing books:

https://bookshop.org/shop/gwft

NOTES